AS REAL AS I GET

C.S. MORROW

authorHOUSE®

AuthorHouse™
1663 Liberty Drive
Bloomington, IN 47403
www.authorhouse.com
Phone: 1-800-839-8640

First published by AuthorHouse 7/22/2009

ISBN: 978-1-4490-0236-7 (sc)

Library of Congress Control Number: 2009906670

Printed in the United States of America
Bloomington, Indiana

This book is printed on acid-free paper.

CONTENTS

When I Think of You

The taste of your lips on mine, then to have them flowing over my skin
Keeps me tossin' and turnin' all night
The scent of you, like perfume on my sheets, compels me to draw these
sheets close and take long, deep breaths of you
Your arms engulfing me as I slumber is what I want most
The remembrance of the passion of your gentle touch—I'm longing to
feel you tonight
The feeling that nothing will ever hurt me makes me want you to stay
and never leave
For you to say you love me and mean it
That's all I really want

Last Night

Last night
I needed someone to hold me
Needed to be near someone
You were that one
But do not think that
There was anything more to it
I have not forgiven you
I have not forgotten
The good or the bad
I can not go back to that
I can not go back to you
But every now and then
I need someone to hold me
Need someone near
You were that one

Slow Hustle

15 years is a long time to be hustlin' but that's what I've been doing
staying up all night, sleeping all day
never punching anybody's clock
white collar crime, blue collar crime
but I've never been collared
never spent a single day in lock up
I've been lucky that way
For so long, I wanted to live a "normal" life
Get a real job, a 9-5
I tried so many times but the streets pay so much better
So I couldn't stay away from it
All that money, all those women

With all the money I've made hustlin' life should be good, now that I'm
serious about going legit
My money should be stacked
One thing about hustlin'---money comes fast...you spend it even faster
because you know you can always earn it back
you never really think about life AFTER the game
I'm realizing now how hard it is to make it
bills are piling up
I can't just walk in the mall on the day the new Jordans come out and
pick up a few pair
I have to wait
I have a budget now
I'm trying to stay straight
trying to leave the game before my luck goes bad
but this shit's so hard
contrary to what people say, you **can** stop the hustle
but why would anyone want to?

Bruno and His Paper

Every Sunday
'round noon, sometimes later
I hear a ring at my door
Bruno's come for his paper

If I don't answer
If I try to ignore
He'll ring again, maybe knock
He's not leavin' 'til I come to the door

$2 is all he wants on Sunday
The next day only 1
He don't accept I.O.U. s
You gotta pay upfront

Don't come with silver or copper
Bruno, he don't like loose change
He'll take it if that's all you got
'Cause after all, he IS a businessman

Bruno will keep his end of the deal
As long as you keep yours
Get your money right Saturday night
Come Sunday, expect him at your door

But

I'm so tired of listening to you talk
every other word is 'but'
I know I need to stop doing this BUT..........
I thought about doing that BUT.................
you have an excuse for **every**thing
nothing's ever your fault
you are to be blamed for nothing
it's all out of your control
poor you
you're so full of it
you want the World and everyone in it to bend to your will
you expect all kinds of concessions and exceptions
certain restrictions always apply with you
I don't know what cloud your head has been stuck in
but you need to peak out long enough to get a glimpse of the real world
the one with REAL people who have REAL problems
the one where everyone struggles to get whatever it is they have
until you realize and accept that nothing is owed to you and you don't
deserve anymore than the rest of us
you'll be nothing more than an excuse maker, an action-faker
when you ought to be an action-taker

Retreat

Whatever happened to that glow in your eyes
The one you used to get when you saw me
Whatever happened to the smiles, the laughter, the hopefulness?
They use you
They hurt you
So badly that you've chosen to retreat from the World and all its trap-
pings ---including me
It was hard for me to open up—but I grew to trust you—so I did it
I opened up, I gave you my heart
Gave you all my love
All I ever did was give
I would have given more but you didn't want it
You didn't want it because you don't want me anymore
You shut down
You shut down and shut me out
I don't really understand why
You offer explanations and apologies but they don't help the hurt
And they won't heal my heart

Time

I want to get away
Run
Fly
Fade
away
everyone's in my ear
I can't get a word in
everyone wants, everyone needs, everyone says
inside my head stirs a symphony of 'what ifs', 'whys' and 'probablys'
I'm not sure of anything
I don't pretend to be
why is everyone looking to me for answers
all I want right now is the one thing I don't have
TIME
Time to Think
Time to Breathe
Time to Pick Things Apart
I have so much catching up to do
I don't know if I ever will
I don't know when or how to start
I want to be happy, I want to find peace
But what I want isn't really important, is it?

Scars

has life gotten you so down
has it beaten you so
that you've just given up? stopped trying?

all your life you've been smothered by negativity
hurt by those closest to you
disappointed by those you've trusted most

everyday will not be a good one
everyone hurts sometimes
but more of your days should be good than bad---are they?
your joys should outshine your pains—do they?

when I look in your eyes there's sadness
constant sadness
when you laugh, you smile---it never leaves you
I can feel the heaviness and loneliness in your heart
as if it were my own

I wish there was some way I could fix it for you
wish I could make you understand
that you are so much more than
better than
so much greater than you believe
you deserve the unconditional, undying love that you've been seeking
all your life
you deserve respect
you deserve to be happy

you CAN get all that you deserve, all that's due you
believe me, you can
all you have to do is try
all you have to do is want it
take that first step, then the next
if you need me to walk with you, hold your hand—I will
if you need me to help navigate---just ask

but I will not force you
I will not drag you, kicking and screaming
I won't attempt to beat you down mentally until you submit

You have to believe that you are deserving
You have to believe that you will succeed
You have to believe in happiness
You have to want it
You have to be ready
You have to believe in yourself the way that I believe in you
Do you believe??

Go Running

I gave you all of me
only for you to throw me a few scraps of you here and there whenever
you felt like it
you wanted to be *The Man*
you wanted to be relied on and needed
so when someone else would call on you, you'd go running
your family, your friends, your ex-
you'd go running
money, a ride, a helping hand---whatever they needed
you were right there
mr. fix-it
I don't need your money and I have my own car
All I wanted was to feel SPECIAL
I wanted to feel like I was important to you
I needed someone to try and understand me
to encourage me
to love me always
to love me unconditionally
you went running
away

I would have done anything for you
but you saw me as a threat because I had no pressing financial need—
no tangible need
you didn't think I needed you
so the time you should have spent loving me was spent loving someone
else
I don't know how many there were and I don't know how long they
lasted
but it was never about me
you were never about me
it was all about you

Bad Terms

I still have visions of you and me
Together
but they're no longer romantic
I see me slashing your tires
raking my fingernails across your face
sometimes
I even think of knifing you
you had no reason to hurt me
you just did
and I don't think you feel bad about it
as much as I have loved you
that's how much I hate you right now

Confirmation

you spent the first 4 years trying to get it
and the next 6 coming back for more
it only stopped when I brought it to an end
you still kept asking
right up until the day you walked to the altar
I always thought you were no good
now I know
Bastard

Relentless

I didn't want to love you
went so far as to tell you so
you persisted
your persistence was profitable
you were able to slip into the most guarded part of me
untied the strings holding my heart together
then stood by while it fell to pieces
while I fell to pieces
you showed no care
acted as if you did not know me
I thought you were wooing me, choosing me
you were actually using me, fooling me
my disbelief was matched only by my devastation
the Devil himself would have been more kind

Impenetrable

Flowers will be thought of as a kind gesture
not a symbol of affection
Gifts will be just that—Gifts
nothing should be read into it
phone calls are ok but time spent must be limited
sex without romance
hugs, no kisses
There's a fortress around my heart and the sentries never sleep
I don't want to be in love

Life

every time I think I've found the answers
every time I think I'm on the right path
I crash into a brick wall or fall through thorny bushes
sticks, stones...they do indeed break bones
and thorned words break hearts
my scars are too numerous
my confusion and frustration profound
I'm ready to exit this intricate maze, this labyrinth we know as life
I can't seem to get it right

Injury

To call at such odd hours—and never from your home
You actually thought I was too stupid to know
THAT was the Insult
Today came the Injury---you married her
6 years
6 years of wanting
6 years of trying to understand you
to end up with nothing
alone
we wouldn't have lasted, I'm sure of it
so it's best you try with someone else
but it stings a little, knowing that you thought so little of me
cared so little
that you didn't even consider the possibility

One Way Love

I waited all night long
You never rang my phone
I got no call from you

I stood out in the snow
You never showed
Why do you do the things you do?

For hours, I paced the floor
You never rapped at my door
I bought new shoes to wear

Gun to my head
In seconds, I'll be dead
All because you never cared

Disbelief

it's so hard to accept
I'm trying hard not to believe
but I can't overlook the facts
can't deny what I've seen

the blood, the bodies, the victims
such a horrifying scene
the pain, suffering and sadness
caused by someone who is incomprehensibly mean

there've been no apologies or pleas for forgiveness
by the perpetrator of these crimes
not even a shameful eye cast down
no remorse of any kind

he is hated by all but one, feared by most—
--he doesn't care
this is the heaviest of all burdens
A Killer's Mother must bear

I do not know *this* person
cuffed, shackled and guarded
I do not know this man
convicted of these charges

I remember a sweet boy, a kind man
Incapable of such cruelty
Someone loved by all who knew him
Someone loved most by me

do I feel guilt or shame for his actions?
I had no hand in his crimes.
Do I disagree with the verdict
He killed so he must die

But know this...I did not raise a killer.....

Instant Autumn

It was 85 degrees yesterday
90 the day before
today my sweater and wool skirt are a must
the mercury continues to drop
today is a soup day
a day to snuggle
the cool days of Fall come too soon

11 Days

December 10th
I love you upon sight and you profess the same
many times
'Thinkin' about you emails
'Whatcha' doin' phone calls
long nights filled with secrets swapping
lots of lovemaking
11 days straight
what happened on the 21st?
my heart is still full but there are no new messages in my inbox
no matter how many times I log on
no voice messages at home or on the cell
I was wishing for a lifetime
All I got was 11 days

Hoping to Find

All my life I've been looking
hoping to find
That Man
the one who'd be   my comfort
                        my strength
                        my inspiration
I would have bet every remaining breath in my breast that it was you
but your kisses became bitter and your touch turned icy
all my life I've been looking
hoping to find

Deep Kiss

Let it happen
Fast, Slow
Either
numbing
Fantastically Orgasmic
Put all your passion into it
Be Lost

Left Hanging

I was gonna give you kisses
was gonna give you kisses and moans
but you never called

Good Cry

I cry
sometimes I know why
sometimes I don't
sadness, hurt, loneliness---it's all here
I keep pushing it back until finally.......
I stop trying
my spirit gets crowded and I allow myself to feel the things I don't
want to
when it's all over I'm a little lighter
I feel freer
I let it go
To make room for all the good things I know will come

Reflection

so desperate for affection
feeling lucky to get whatever you gave -- no matter how little
wanting more
but not believing I had a right to expect it
I was too busy being too afraid of being alone to realize that
I knew you didn't care about me
you saw me catch a glimpse from time to time
but you never thought I'd see
did you?
I'm seeing the light that you tried so hard to extinguish and I've fallen
madly in love with myself
I deserve respect, peace and genuine joy every day of my Life
I'm wonderful
and beautiful
Radiant, even
worthy of so much more than you've ever given me

Blue

It's not nighttime but it's dark
everything is still
the sun is not bright
the clouds are not white
it's as if the whole world has been soaked in tar
including me
that's just how blue I am

Murder on my Mind

what do you do when murder is on your mind?
do you pray to God that these feelings depart?
but how *can* they when the source of such evil, the focus of your hatred
is ever present
should I ask for forgiveness?
what's to forgive?
I've done nothing wrong
not yet
maybe I'll just do it and be done with it
no
I **will** do it
those who commit such crimes cannot be permitted to live
I'm no exception
we die together tonight

As Real as I Get

I'm not a hooker or a whore but I do like to fuck
the kissing, the caressing
heavy breathing, undressing
sucking my tits
licking my clit
I get too hot
I like it on top
bite my ear
smack my rear
drenched in sweat
grab my neck
the steady thrusts
the orgasmic rush
like I said—I'm not a hooker or a whore
but I do like to fuck

Terror

what was that noise?
was it real?
was I dreaming?
I knew I shouldn't have slept with these windows open
I'm terrified
scared to move—but I ave to close these windows
it takes more courage than I ever thought I had to open these blinds
there's no telling what's on the other side
quickly...I close them
but what if someone's already in?
let's get some light in here
closet check
bed check
bathroom check
all clear
lights off
but I still can't sleep
I'm shaking inside and out
Damn, I'm scared

Dave

You weren't the coolest guy in the room
You weren't the most popular with the young ladies
but from the second I saw you I knew you'd be the most special man in
my life
because you were my first sweetheart, my heart was still in one piece
I loved you fearlessly and I was happier than I'd ever been
When I met you, David, I was too young to know very much
But I knew I loved you like I would no other

Charles

Good or bad, you were grateful for all of life's experiences
you were the only person I know who savored every second you were
allowed to live
you were happy to be alive and it showed
that's what made you special to me
even when you saw the darkness approaching you did not surrender
you had to be taken by Force
and what Force it took!
we never had a physical love but every part of me loved every part of
you
my love for you will remain fierce for as long as I shall live
I miss you, Charles

Few Minutes More

she asks him to stay a few minutes more
she sits him down and tells him to relax
she needs to sit close enough to see her reflection in his eyes
so she puts one leg on either side of his
she eases down
puts his face in her hands
closes his eyes
pours a kiss for him that's sweeter than molasses and twice as slow
she tells him he's free to go
he asks to stay

Classified

SBF, mid-20's seeks SM, 25-35
must be disease free, drug free, non-smoker
occasional drink ok
abusers, bi-sexuals, liars, players, unemployeds need not apply
must be able to hold intelligent conversation w/o expletives
college degree not mandatory but must be hard working
must be willing to accept responsibility for his actions and admit when
he's wrong
No Bullshitters, please
should be somewhat spontaneous and creative
must have an open mind but be willing to stand up for what he believes
in
can't be afraid of a strong woman
if qualified and interested, please call

Yearning

Calling out to you in the dark
Trying to calm my restless heart

Hurting because my heart still yearns
Fearing that you'll never return

Remembering our yesterdays
Wondering why you didn't stay

Thinking about how it used to be
Cursing the Sandman because I do not sleep

Loving you 365 days
Needing you in every way

Wanting our memories to leave my dreams
Praying you'll come back to me

After Dark

I see you
you don't even know that I'm watching but I see you
I sit by my window and secretly send you on your way each day and I
greet you when you return
I see who comes, who goes and who stays
Especially who stays
she denies leaving that rose on your bed but you don't believe her
you think she did it
I was the one who put it there
while you slept
I had to be near you
we work in the same building, on the same floor, for the same company
I make it a point to pass you in the hall at least once
every
single
day
I pay more attention to you than even you do
I can tell you what you've worn every day for the past 3 months and 4
days..right down to the cologne
I know what you eat, what you buy, where you go and who you go with
I make it my business to know everything about you
soon, I'll reveal myself
then you'll love me just as much as I love you
I know you will
I know what you're thinking
but I'm not crazy
I really do love you
You need to understand something

I've invested a lot of time and energy into this relationship
so I won't accept anything less than your total devotion
that's the least you can do
nothing will stand in the way of our love
NOTHING
Farewell for now, My Love
I'll see you soon

Kisses and Lies

Kisses and Lies
That's all you ever gave
Kisses and Lies
One
Or the other
One
Then another
Kisses and Lies

People Watching

On any given day
In any given place
A myriad of people pass by
It's amazing how different we are
How different we can feel
Every now and then I sit and watch
Wondering what's in the minds of people passing by
That man in the grey suit—is he smiling because he's a new daddy
Or is that smile the only thing that keeps him from breaking down
Where did her blank stare come from?
Is she confused, indifferent or what?
Is anyone watching me?

New Name

I'm searching for a new name
Not just any name
It will be a gift from my forever lover
I will accept his gift only if it comes with the promise of fidelity and
kindness
In return for his gift
I will give him precious little ones who will share our name
My new family
My new life
will be built upon
my new name

All I Know

I didn't mean to hurt you
That was not my intent

I only wanted you to be strong
strong like me
I wanted to be taken care of
as all women do

but you'd never learned to stand
you were never taught

my strength seemed to weaken you more
I'm sorry
it's all I know

I C U

broken bodies
wails of sorrow
this ward is full of them
as emotionless as I try to be
I can't help but cry sometimes
because I know that most who enter will not exit
at least not on their terms
Death--she frequents this place
she's expected everyday, oftimes welcomed
but it's so hard to get used to her
some may call what I do noble
I don't
it's just necessary

Afterthought

for me, it was a given
that caring, sharing thoughtfulness—and all other things rosy—would
be what we were about
I never dreamed you'd be so in love with yourself
that you could be so selfish, uncaring and cold
it's apparent I'm an afterthought, not your first thought
not even your second
Me, Me, Me
is all you
See, See, See
who knew?
I guess I thought too little and assumed too much

Separated

Are you really?
Is that why her name is still on your answering machine?
Why you only call me from the office or on the road?
Know what I think?
You're not separated from your wife at all
You're a slut like almost every other man
And I hate you
So separate yourself from me!

Snapshot

Someone should take my picture right now
From the front and all sides
Capture my entire face

On another day I'll look at the picture
I want to see if I look any thing at all like I feel today
I'm sad—I miss a few special people that have passed
A little lonely---I don't have a 'special someone'
Ashamed--I've treated someone who cares for me very badly
Just because
Angry—I've been wronged. It doesn't matter who did it.
Lucky—I have caring friends, a loving family
Happy—I have so many of the things I've always wanted. Nice home,
car, clothes.....and I can't forget the shoes!
Thankful—for my health, my strength, my somewhat sound mind
Unappreciated—I give, I do my best, but everybody still screams for
more
I'm just so overwhelmed by so many emotions
I feel like nothing

Does any or all of this show on my face?

Cotton sheets

thread count – 800
color – violet
soft
inviting
once crisp
now wrinkled and folded all around us
springtime fresh before
perfumed with the scent of us now
stroking our bodies as we stroke each other
almost as close to me as you are
I love my cotton sheets

S i g n s

Yield	**it'll never work**
No U Turn	a girl can change her mind, can't she?
SLOW DOWN	NOT READY
Slippery when wet	**my personal fave**
One way	that's right. My Way.
Stop	not a chance

So Sad

Sad?
Yes, I am
But don't waste your pity on me
I'm not a virgin miserable
I've been here many times before
I know the ropes
I'm down now. Way down, in fact
I'll get up, go on and be fine. When it's time.
Leave me to myself
In my misery
It's not so sad that I'm so sad

Casual

you're not special
privileged, yes
but not special
not to me, anyway
there was no "connection"
it was just an act
a physical need was satisfied
it meant nothing
you me nothing
not to me, anyway

Recognize

You say that you've taken my man?
And you're the one he's fucking now?
Let me ask you this
When you are "fucking" him does he say anything?
He may moan a little or grunt some
But does he cry like a hungry infant?
Does every muscle in his body contract so hard that he can't move?
No?
Have you ever denied him your body? After you did this, did he just
accept 'no' and walk away?
Did he politely ask you again?
Or did he beg for just a taste of your sweetness
Would he do or say anything you wanted just to let him put it in?
Didn't think so.
Does he follow you around like a lost puppy, hoping to be fortunate
enough to catch a whiff of you?
Of course not.
You seem shocked that I would say such things with a straight face
I can do this because I've known all along what you've just learned
You may be fucking him
But he'll always be mine
Remember that.

Keep the Funk

those with so little pigment
want Tiger to give the green back
and they talk cold shit about the Goddess herself, Venus
they won't admit it
but they're still hanging on to that 'Massa Mentality'
"keep the Niggers in their place"
those are "their" sports
Meanwhile, we sit back and watch while they steal the Funk-
right in front of our faces
boys named Bubba laying down hip-hop tracks
Latina chicks singing the word 'Nigger' like it's ok
and we're shaking our asses and bobbing our heads
am I supposed to think some blonde haired kid is cool because he
speaks rehearsed ebonics?
am I supposed to be impressed by some teen from the 'burbs mastering
a few simple dance steps?
Whatever, man-
they tried to take jazz, stole Rock & Roll
are we about to hand over hip-hop and R & B?

The. End.

I'll say it again
I Don't Love You
I wanted to be in love and you were near
So I made myself believe I loved you
I was more believable than I imagined I could be
How unfortunate for you
Now, Believe This
You and Me/We
That's all past
All that's left is you
All there is — is me